How To Be A Super Bear

Seven stories to inspire children to grow up to be the very best they can be

by

Grandpa Super Bear

Illustrated by Daniela Frongia

How To Be A Super Bear

Seven stories to inspire children to
grow up to be the very best they can be

by

Grandpa Super Bear

Illustrated by Daniela Frongia

© Copyright 2011

All rights reserved. No part of this publication may be reproduced or
transmitted in any form or by any means, electronic, mechanical,
photocopying, recording, scanning or otherwise, without the
permission in writing of The Publisher.

The name Grandpa Super Bear is a Trade Mark.

Published by
Bruce King - Crown House Publishing
23 Southerton Way | Radlett | Hertfordshire WD7 9LJ | United Kingdom

T: 44 (0)1923 859977   **E:** post@grandpasuperbear.com   **Web:** www.grandpasuperbear.com

ISBN 978 0 9570977 0 4

Printed through
SS Media Ltd
Cardinal Point | Park Road | Rickmansworth | Hertfordshire WD3 1RE | United Kingdom

Contents & Story Summaries

🐾 An important message to anyone reading this book to a child 7

🐾 Grandpa Super Bear introduces himself to Georgie 9

🐾 **Story 1:** Life is magical and anything is possible 13

🐾 **Story 2:** You really can learn to do anything you want to do 17

🐾 **Story 3:** When you are grown, you can be anything you want to be 23

🐾 **Story 4:** There is no such thing as failure 29

🐾 **Story 5:** Why whom you spend the most time playing with is important 33

🐾 **Story 6:** Why you should be very kind to other people 37

🐾 **Story 7:** How to enjoy every single day 43

An important message to parents, grandparents, aunts, uncles, teachers, friends and indeed anyone who is reading these words to a child...

This is a book that is best read at bedtime but can of course also be read at any other time of the day. It is not intended to be read through at one sitting. One chapter at a time is probably enough for most children unless whomever you are reading it to wants you to carry on.

Each story will set them on a journey of excellence, inspire them to be the very best they can be, and to become a very precious person on Planet Earth.

Each story plants seeds of wisdom into the minds of wonderful little people who are uninhibited, eager to learn and are wondrous of the world we live in.

Enjoy reading this to someone dear to you who will soon become a Super Bear!

With much love and bear hugs

Grandpa Super Bear

Georgie was having an afternoon nap...

Outside the window, someone was gently tapping away, tap, tap, tap against the glass.

Georgie woke up and there, floating just outside his window, was a bear with a flying cape, the initials GSB on his belt in big gold letters and funny stripy socks.

Georgie had never seen anything floating outside his window before, except of course a bird. Georgie was most puzzled but not in the least bit scared. Whoever it was that was floating out there looked so cuddly, kind, wise and friendly.

Open the window please said the cuddly floating bear and Georgie did just that. The cuddly bear floated in and sat down.

Hello he said. I am Grandpa Super Bear and I have come to teach you how to become a Super Bear, just like me. I am going to come back to see you from time to time, so whenever I tap, tap, tap on the window, always let me in. Will you do that please?

'Yes I will Grandpa Super Bear' said Georgie.

Great! Awesome! Fantasmagorical! First of all, let me tell you a little about me and where I come from.

I come from a place called Planet Bear. Planet Bear is very much like the Planet Earth that you live on except that on my planet we are all called Bears. We also look like Bears.

I have been watching you grow up for a while and I really like you. So from now on, I am going to call you a Little Bear, just like all the other little children on Planet Bear.

Once upon a time, before you were born, you were living in your Mummy's tummy.

On Planet Bear, little people who have not been born yet are called Soon Bears.

As soon as they are born, they become Baby Bears. Then, as they grow up, they become Little Bears and then Teen Bears and eventually, all sorts of different Bears.

Some will grow up to be very clever Smart Bears and Super Bears. Others who are not so fortunate will become Soppy Bears or Grumpy Bears.

Some will become Happy Bears and Funny Bears and all sorts of other Bears.

Some will grow up to be a mixture of these.

I have come to help you to be the most Super Bear you can possibly be. So here is a very important thing for you to know Georgie.

I was not always a Super Bear. Many years ago I was a Little Bear, just like you. I was not born with any more super powers than you. We are all born with super powers, but most people do not learn how to use them. In fact many Little Bears become Soppy Bears and remain Soppy Bears most of their lives. But we are not going to let that happen to you are we Little Bear?

It took me a long time to develop my super powers and become a Super Bear because I had to learn so many things. But you will not have to wait very long at all because you have me to teach you now.

So you can be a Super Bear faster than you might ever imagine is possible. You do want to be a Super Bear don't you?

'Yes please. I really do' said Georgie.

I thought you would. So here is your first lesson.

The first thing I want to teach you Georgie, is that life is magical and anything is possible…

Yes – life is indeed magical Little Bear. That is why I have put on my Magician's hat and picked up my magic wand. Because life is magical, almost anything is possible. You see it all depends upon how you look at things.

Have you ever seen a real live elephant fly? I do not mean the elephants in cartoons. I mean real live elephants like you see in the zoo or on safari in Africa or India.

I do not suppose you have seen one fly and neither have I. It is impossible because elephants do not have wings and without wings, elephants cannot fly. Not even if they flap those big ears very fast. Neither can giraffes, or hippos or cats or dogs or any other animals that do not have wings. Neither can you fly Little Bear, because you do not have wings either or a magic cloak like mine.

But is it impossible?

It is not!

Grandpa Super Bear How To Be A Super Bear 13

Once upon a time on Planet Bear, a Grumpy Bear heard me telling some Little Bears that I could make elephants and giraffes and hippos and cats and dogs and other animals fly. He said I was a silly old Grandpa Super Bear. So I decided to show him that I could make them fly, and without using my magic wand.

I went to the Zoo to see my good friend the Zookeeper Bear.

I borrowed some elephants and giraffes and hippos and cats and dogs. I put them in a truck and drove them to the airport.

Then I put them in an airplane, I started the engines and the airplane flew into the sky.

And the animals without wings were flying. You would have been flying too if you had been with them Little Bear.

So when anyone tells you that something is impossible, there might always be a way of making it possible. That is how Super Bears think.

As you get older, some Grumpy Bears and Soppy Bears will tell you that lots of things are impossible and you should not try to do them.

They might tell you that you are not big enough, or small enough, not clever enough or brave enough, not strong enough or old enough, or you do not have the right tools.

They might tell you that nobody has done it before and give you all sorts of other reasons why you cannot do something.

Whenever that happens, remember that Super Bears believe that almost anything is possible. Super Bears like you and I will always find a way to achieve what we want, no matter what others may say.

So whenever someone tells you that something is impossible, just ask yourself this…

'What would Grandpa Super Bear do?'

If you think about it long enough, you are sure to find an answer – almost as if by magic.

Will you do that for me Little Bear?

'Yes I will Grandpa Super Bear' said Georgie.

Well done! You are already well on your way to becoming a Super Bear. Now go back to sleep and I will come and see you again very soon. Have sweet dreams.

Grandpa Super Bear leaned forward and whispered 'Good night Little Bear' and Georgie reached out and stroked Grandpa Super Bear's warm furry coat. It felt so lovely and soft.

Georgie drifted off to sleep feeling warm and safe and very happy indeed.

Tap, tap, tap – here I am again Little Bear…

Georgie heard the tap, tap, tapping and opened the window. Grandpa Super Bear floated in and sat down on the windowsill. Georgie was so excited to see him again and laughed a lot at Grandpa Super Bear's stripy socks.

Hello again Little Bear. The reason I have come to see you today is to explain to you that you really can learn to do anything you want to do.

Throughout your life there could be a gazillion things you might want to do. You might want to learn how to drive a car, or fly an aeroplane, or drive a train, or even a fire engine and make the bells ring while you are driving along.

You may want to make a movie, write a book, or paint a picture. You might want to build a tree house or even a real house.

You might want to make your own computer, or a telescope to see Planet Bear and the other planets and stars.

You may want to build a go-kart, or a bicycle or a kite to fly in the sky and all kinds of other things.

You might even want to wrestle with alligators, although I do not recommend that as it could be very dangerous. I know that for sure because I tried it once myself and the alligator bit my back side. But I survived. But some people do wrestle with alligators and could teach you how if you really wanted to.

So this is what I want you to learn today. It is that you can really and truly do anything you want to do. That is a Grandpa Super Bear promise and I keep all my promises.

Of course some people will tell you something different. What they do not understand is that somebody else has already done almost anything that they think it is not possible to do.

Whatever it is you decide you want to do and no matter how difficult you or other people think it is, there is always someone, somewhere who has already done it or is working on how to do it.

Super Bears also like to help other people and there are lots of other Super Bears who will help you too. You could ask your mother or father, your grandpa or grandma, your aunts and uncles.

You could ask your friends and their friends and you could ask your teachers. If you ask enough people you will almost certainly find someone who knows how to teach you.

When you cannot find a Super Bear, you can also learn from books and magazines. All books and magazines are written by Super Bears.

You can go to the library and find a book or magazine on almost any subject on the planet. You can surf the Internet on a computer or on a mobile telephone.

You can watch programs on the television. Whatever it is you want to learn how to do, someone, somewhere has written down everything you need to know. When you start searching for answers Little Bear, you might even discover something else even more exciting you might want to do.

That reminds me that once upon a time on Planet Bear there was a little girl bear called Hannah Bear. Ever since she was a Little Bear, Hannah Bear had always wanted to learn to ballet dance.

She read books on ballet dancing, she watched films of ballet dancers and she dreamed about dancing herself. Often she would dance around the house pretending to be a famous ballet dancer.

One day, Hannah Bear was surfing on the Internet, looking at ballet shoes. She looked at so many pages and then came across a picture of a pretty lady bear who was wearing ballet shoes and was walking across a tightrope. It was stretched between two poles, high up in a circus tent.

Hannah had discovered something different and from that day on, Hannah Bear wanted to learn to be a tightrope walker instead of a ballet dancer. I am very pleased to tell you that when she became a Teen Bear, she went to one of the best Tightrope Schools on Planet Bear and learned to be the very best tight rope walker in the school.

Now Little Bear, it is time for you to make me a promise. Promise me that you really and truly believe you can do whatever you want to do. Do you promise me that?

Well done. Will you also promise me that when you are a Super Bear like me, you will also help teach other Little Bears how to be Super Bears?

'I promise I will Grandpa Super Bear' said Georgie.

That is wonderful. It is time to go to sleep now and have some lovely dreams.

Dream about all the different things you might want to do when you are a Super Bear.

I will see you soon.

Grandpa Super Bear stroked Georgie's head and said goodnight and Georgie quickly fell into a deep sleep and dreamed wonderful dreams.

Would you like to make a list of some of the things you would like to do when you are a Super Bear?

When you have thought about this some more, write them down here please Little Bear.

Tap, tap, tap – it's me again Little Bear…

Georgie opened the window and Grandpa Super Bear floated in wearing yet another pair of stripy socks.

Hello again Little Bear. May I sit in your little chair please? It looks so comfortable.

'Of course you can' said Georgie.

Thank you said Grandpa Super Bear.

Today I am here to tell you that when you are a grown up Super Bear, you can be anything you want to be.

I don't suppose you have thought a lot about what you want to be when you are grown up, but it is never too soon to start thinking about it Little Bear.

Maybe you want to grow up to be an actor or actress in films or in the theatre or on the television, or even all three. You may want to be a doctor or a dentist or an optician or a nurse. You may want to be an artist or a builder or a racing driver or a magician. You may even want to be a lawyer or a judge or even a prime minister or a president.

There are just so very many things you could learn to be and no matter what other people may tell you, I promise you that you can learn how to be anything you want to be. The choice is yours and yours alone.

In order to be anything you want to be, you usually have to go to school and learn about it.

You start by learning some very basic things like learning to read and write and to do some simple arithmetic – some children and their teachers call them sums. Then as you get older, you learn about more and more things, and very soon you become a Super Bear.

When you are a Super Bear, you start to get even more ideas on what you would like to be when you grow up and you realise that there are even more choices than you ever imagined before. Then you can go to special schools that will teach you everything you need to know to become whatever you want to be.

Do you want to have the choice of being anything that you want to be?

'Yes - I really do' said Georgie.

Great! So here is what you must do. You must not be a lazy Little Bear! You must be a smart Little Bear and listen to what your teachers teach you. Listen carefully to the teachers through all the lessons they give you and even the lessons you do not like quite so much. Read your books and study well. Do your homework and learn everything you need to know.

If you do that, one day very soon you will be a Super Bear and you can be whatever you want to be. That is another Grandpa Super Bear promise.

That reminds me of a Little Bear on Planet Bear called Gilbert Bear. He came to talk to me one day because he really did not know what he wanted to be when he grew up. I promised to help him decide.

We sat down and chatted for a while and I suggested he made a list of all the different things he might want to be.

By the time he had finished the list, Gilbert had thirty different things written down. 'Goodness me' he said. 'How will I choose which one Grandpa Super Bear?'

Well here is the most important thing to think about, I said. When you have to go to work every day, it is nice to do something you really love to do. The more you love it and the more excited you are by it, the less like work and the more like fun it will seem to be.

Go down the list slowly and carefully. Think about each one and then decide which you would love to be doing most of all and the one that excites you the most of all. Take the list home and do that. I promise you the answer will come to you.

Gilbert Bear came back to see me the following day. I asked him if he had made up his mind. 'Yes I have Grandpa Super Bear', he said. 'The thing I would like to do most of all is to help other Bears get well when they become Sick Bears. So I have decided I am going to be a Doctor Bear.'

Gilbert Bear studied hard at school. Then he went to a special school for people who wanted to be Doctor Bears and several years later, he passed his exams and became a very good Doctor Bear indeed.

So when you are deciding what you want to be when you grow up, you too must think of what you would love most of all and what would excite you most of all. Will you do that please Little Bear?

'I will Grandpa Super Bear' said Georgie.

Well done. Now that is enough for today Little Bear. It is time to go to sleep and dream about all the things you could grow up to be when you are a Super Bear.

Sleep tight and I will see you soon.

'Goodnight Grandpa Super Bear', whispered Georgie and drifted off to sleep dreaming about Gilbert the Doctor Bear.

Would you like to make a list of some of the things you would like to be when you are a Super Bear?

When you have thought about this some more, write them down here please Little Bear.

_____

_____

_____

_____

_____

_____

_____

_____

_____

Tap, tap, tap – I am back again Little Bear…

Georgie had left the window open for Grandpa Super Bear hoping he would come today. So Grandpa Super Bear floated straight in and sat right down in Georgie's chair.

Hello Little Bear. Today I have come to teach you there is no such thing as failure.

'That sounds very interesting. Please tell me more' said Georgie.

Once upon a time, many years ago on your Planet Earth, people did not flick a switch and turn on a light. Instead, they had to light candles or oil lamps so they could see in the dark.

The man who invented the light bulb was called Thomas Edison. He was an inventor who made 1,000 unsuccessful attempts at inventing the light bulb before he finally made one that worked. Imagine that! It took him a very long time.

When someone asked Mr. Edison, 'How did it feel to fail 1,000 times?' he replied, 'I didn't fail 1,000 times. The light bulb was an invention with 1,000 steps to making it work.'

So was Thomas Edison a soppy person who failed 1,000 times or was he a smart person who would not give up until he had done his super best?

You bet he was a super smart person Little Bear! He never gave up.

Also, many years ago on Planet Earth, there was no such thing as an airplane. But two brothers called Wilbur and Orville Wright were watching birds fly one day and decided that they would try to build something that could fly like a bird and carry a person in it. They decided to call it an airplane.

They built their first airplane over one hundred years ago. It crashed and broke into pieces.

They tried and tried again and built many more airplanes.

Every one of those crashed and broke into pieces too. Sometimes they got badly hurt in the crash.

It was five years before they made an airplane that flew safely for more than five minutes.

Because of what they invented, you can now fly around the world and visit places people could never visit before.

Were they soppy to keep trying or were they super smart Little Bear?

You got it! They were indeed super smart. Without them and their decision to never give up, we may not have airplanes today.

When someone asked Wilbur Wright how it felt to fail so many times, he said – 'We never failed. We just discovered lots of ways an airplane would not fly and then we finally discovered the way they would fly'.

There are going to be times, maybe many times, when you try to do something and you cannot make it work Little Bear.

The lesson in this story is that there is no such thing as failing, unless of course you give up and never try again. So whenever you try to do something and it does not work, never, ever give up. Super Bears will always find a way.

So what are you going to do when things do not work out as you would like, the first time, or the next time, or the time after that Little Bear?

Will you be a Super Bear and try and try again Georgie?

'Of course I will' said Georgie.

Great stuff! You really are going to be a Super Bear.

I think that is quite enough for tonight. It is time to go to sleep now. I will see you soon. Dream about all the wonderful things you are going to do when you are a Super Bear.

Good night Little Bear.

'Good night Grandpa Super Bear' said Georgie. 'Please come back and see me again soon.'

Of course I will said Grandpa Super Bear.

Georgie fell asleep right away and dreamed super dreams.

Tap, tap, tap – are you there Little Bear?

Georgie opened the window and Grandpa Super Bear floated in and sat down in his favourite chair.

Hello Little Bear. Today I want to talk to you about why it is important which Little Bears you spend the most time playing with.

When you spend a lot of time playing with soppy children, some of their soppiness can rub off on you and you can become soppy too. We don't want that do we? No indeed we do not!

When you spend a lot of time playing with grumpy children, some of their grumpiness can rub off on you. Then you become grumpy too. We don't want that either do we?

Now I am not saying you should never play with soppy people or grumpy people because we must learn to have a good time and get on well with all kinds of people.

But the more time you spend playing with smart children and super children and happy children, the more you will become like them. And you do want to be super, smart and happy don't you Little Bear?

What I am teaching you, reminds me of something else that happened once upon a time on Planet Bear. Once upon a time there was a six-year-old called Jimmy Bear. He was a nice, friendly and very polite Little Bear who was respectful to his parents and his teachers and was a very Happy Bear.

But after school, Jimmy started mixing with a gang of very Rough Bears and Angry Bears and Rude Bears.

They would shout a lot, fight a lot and generally make a nuisance of themselves.

They were a gang of Bad Little Bears.

After just a short while of playing with this gang of Bad Bears, Jimmy Bear become rough and angry and rude too.

His teachers complained to his parents he was not doing his school work.

His parents complained to the teachers that he was being angry and rude at home.

They were blaming each other for Jimmy Bear's bad behavior.

Grandpa Super Bear had been keeping a watchful eye on Jimmy Bear and decided to tell Jimmy's parents what they should do. He told them about an after school club that Jimmy could go to which was called The Smart Bears Play Club.

Everyone who went there was the same age or nearly the same age as Jimmy Bear and they were all being taught to be Super Bears. So Jimmy was sent there every day for a little while after school and had no time to play with the gang of Bad Little Bears.

The teachers were very kind and played lots of interesting games with all the Little Bears. They read stories together and went for walk and studied nature. They went on trips to the zoo and museums and lots of other very interesting places.

Can you guess what happened next?

You got it Little Bear. After just a short while, Jimmy Bear turned back into a nice, friendly and very polite Little Bear. The more he went to the Smart Bears Play Club, the smarter and happier he became. His teachers and parents were also happy too and everyone lived happily ever after.

That is more than enough to think about for today. It is time to go to sleep now. Dream about all the nice, friendly, polite and Smart Bears you are going to play with in the future and have fun in your dreams.

I will see you soon Little Bear. Goodbye for now.

'Goodbye Grandpa Super Bear' said Georgie.

Grandpa Super Bear gave Georgie a gentle kiss goodnight on the forehead, left quietly through the window and closed it behind him.

Georgie fell asleep right away and dreamed of all the fun the Little Bears had in the Smart Bears Play Club.

6. Tap, tap, tap – here I am again Little Bear…

Georgie jumped off the bed and opened the window. He was so excited to see Grandpa Super Bear again.

Grandpa Super Bear flew in through the window and plopped himself down in the chair.

'So what have you come to teach me today?' asked Georgie.

Little Bear, today I have come to teach you that it is really important you are very kind to other people.

All the planets that people live on everywhere are round in shape. One of the reasons they are round is because of a universal law which goes like this:

'What goes around, comes around'

If you have not heard this expression before,
you will hear smart people say it many times in the future. This is what it means.

If somebody does something horrible to somebody else, eventually something horrible will happen to them. Because what goes around, comes around.

If somebody takes something that does not belong to them from someone else, eventually somebody will take something from them. Because what goes around, comes around.

And if somebody is unkind to someone else, then it is almost certain that eventually, someone will be unkind to them. Why is that Little Bear?

You got it! Because what goes around comes around.

So here is what I want you to do Little Bear. I would like you to be kind to all other people please. Do nice things for them.

Help them to do things they cannot do for themselves.
Be considerate to other people when they are feeling unhappy or grumpy. By being kind to them, you will make them feel happy and you will feel happy too because what goes around always comes around.

Talking to you about this reminds me of something else that happened on Planet Bear.

Once upon a time there was a Grumpy Old Bear called Ebenezer Bear. He lived all by himself in a little house in a little street in a little town called Hard To Find. I am sure you can guess why it was called Hard To Find can't you Little Bear?

Ebenezer Bear was grumpy with all his neighbors. He complained every day to Janet Bear who lived next door about her dog barking at him. He shouted at Jack Bear who lived two doors away about Jack Bear's cat scratching at his front door.

He sent nasty little notes to Brenda Bear who lived opposite him because her parrot squawked in the middle of the night and woke him up. He telephoned Raymond Bear who lived next door to Brenda Bear and complained that Raymond's hens went 'cock a doodle doo' very loudly every morning at five o clock and woke him up.

Ebenezer Bear was grumpy with so many people that nobody wanted to talk to him. Nobody wanted to invite him in for a cup of Honey Bear Tea and nobody wanted to visit him for a friendly chat. As well as being a very Grumpy Bear, he was also a very Lonely Bear.

Grandpa Super Bear felt very sorry for Ebenezer Bear and decided to see if I could help. I told him that if he were to just stop being so grumpy and stop complaining to everyone, just for a short while, he might see some very nice changes in the way people behaved towards him.

I also told him that if he smiled at everyone he met and did a few kind things for them like helping them in with their shopping, stroking their cats and dogs and maybe even helping to tidy up the hen's house from time to time, that he might see some almost magical changes.

Ebenezer Bear agreed to do as Grandpa Bear suggested and see what happened and if anything changed.

He was very pleased indeed. Soon after he stopped complaining and started smiling and doing nice things for his neighbors, some very strange things started happening.

The dog stopped barking at him. The cat stopped scratching his door. The parrot stopped squawking quite so loudly and did not wake him up and the hens woke up every morning at five o clock but they whispered cock a doodle doo instead of crowing out loud.

Not only that, but when he smiled at other people, they smiled back and said nice things to him. Before very long, everyone in the street was talking about how much Ebenezer Bear had changed.

They invited him in for tea. They came round to visit him for a chat and sometimes even bought him nice things to eat with his tea.

Ebenezer Bear had stopped being a Grumpy Bear and had become a Happy Bear and everyone in Hard To Find Town lived happily ever after.

So you see that one of the easiest ways to make other people feel happy is to say nice things to them, do nice things for them and smile. When you smile, what goes around comes around very quickly indeed. When you smile at another person, you feel happy too – right away.

So give me a big smile, close your eyes, go to sleep and dream happy dreams Little Bear.

Georgie smiled a very big smile, leaned forward to stroke Grandpa Super Bear's soft, furry face, and then lay down and fell asleep right away.

Tap, tap, tap – I am back again Little Bear…

Hello Little Bear said Grandpa Super Bear as he floated in through the open window.

'Hello Grandpa Super Bear' said Georgie. 'What are you going to teach me today? I have been so looking forward to seeing you.'

Today Little Bear, I want to explain to you that it is so very important to enjoy every single day.

When I walk along the street on Planet Earth, I see a lot more grumpy faces than I see smiley faces. I see so many people rushing to and fro, looking at their watches and huffing and puffing and scratching their heads with worry. It is a shame that they probably never had someone like Grandpa Super Bear to teach them to enjoy every day, no matter what they have to do and where they have to go.

This is what I want you to know Little Bear. Every day can be and should be full of happiness and joy. We are also very fortunate that we do not have to rely on anyone else to make it happy and joyful. It is entirely up to us because we can choose how we want to feel.

Let me explain to you how this works by telling you another story about something else that happened on Planet Bear.

Once upon a time there were two Teen Bears sitting on a bench in Bear Fun Park enjoying the sunshine and admiring the flowers. One was called Helen Bear and the other was called Tom Bear.

All of a sudden a big dark cloud came across the sky, covered up the sun and then started to pour down millions of raindrops.

Tom Bear was very upset. 'I do not like this', he said to Helen Bear. 'I'm getting wet, the water is running down my face and down my neck and I'm feeling very uncomfortable. I do not like clouds, I do not like rain, I do not like sitting in the wet and I am going to have to walk through puddles and wet grass all the way home. What a horrible day this has turned out to be'.

With that he got up and trudged across the wet grass and through the puddles muttering away to himself all the way home.

What a Soppy Bear, Helen thought to herself. I love the rain. It is cool and refreshing and if feels like lots of tickly little fingers running down my face and down my neck.

The grass is sparkling like there are a million tiny stars lighting it up and it looks so much greener and nicer now. The flowers are getting lots to drink and will be bigger and brighter when I come back tomorrow. How joyful it is to see the rain.

I shall go home soon and I shall have such fun walking through the wet grass and jumping in the puddles and making a splash.

Then Helen hopped and skipped and splashed in puddles and sang songs to herself all the way home.

So you see Little Bear, Tom chose to be a Miserable Bear and Helen chose to be a Happy Bear. Now you understand what I mean when I say you can choose how you want to feel.

Even when bad things happen, which they sometimes do, you can choose not let them upset you for more than a few seconds before you decide to find some happiness in the situation. There is always so much to be happy about and it is so much more fun being a Happy Bear than a Miserable Bear.

Promise me you will be a Happy Little Bear and enjoy every single day. Will you do that Little Bear?

'Yes I will ' said Georgie.

You really are a Super Little Bear. It will be a while before I see you again, and until I do, you should know that I am always thinking about you and keeping a watch over you. How about a big hug with Grandpa Super Bear?

Georgie gave Grandpa Super Bear a very, very big hug and stroked his lovely soft, warm fur.

'Please do come back and see me again soon Grandpa Super Bear' Georgie said.

Of course I will. Good night Little Super Bear. I love you very much.

Here is one last thing for you to do when you have some time Little Super Bear.

You have probably noticed that Grandpa Super Bear loves wearing brightly coloured, stripy socks. So would you like to design a sock for me? Color this in and make it bright and fun please.

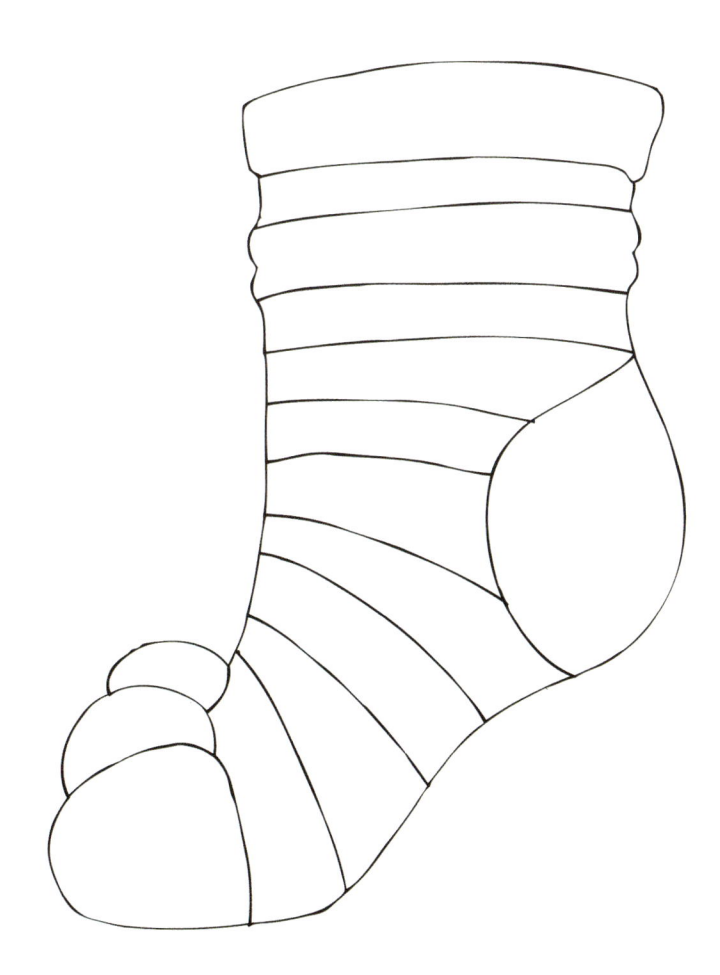